Pebble® Plus

Physical Science

Electricity

by Abbie Dunne

raintree

a Capstone company — publishers for children

Raintree is an imprint of Capstone Global Library Limited, a company incorporated in England and Wales having its registered office at 264 Banbury Road, Oxford, OX2 7DY – Registered company number: 6695582

www.raintree.co.uk
myorders@raintree.co.uk

Edited by Linda Staniford
Designed by Veronica Scott
Picture research by Eric Gohl
Production by Katy LaVigne

ISBN 978 1 474 72244 5
20 19 18 17 16
10 9 8 7 6 5 4 3 2 1

British Library Cataloguing in Publication Data
A full catalogue record for this book is available from the British Library.

Acknowledgements
We would like to thank the following for permission to reproduce photographs:
iStockphoto: Jolka100, 19; Science Source: GIPhotoStock, 21; Shutterstock: ArtisticPhoto, 7, chungking, 9, Designua, 11, Gregg Cerenzio, 5, Iakov Filimonov, 15, Its Design, 11 (power plant), Oleksiy Mark, 17, ULKASTUDIO, 13, Vitaly Korovin, cover

Design Elements: Shutterstock

Contents

What is electricity?

Electricity is a kind of energy. Tiny particles called electrons carry energy. The moving electrons make energy to light lamps and run motors.

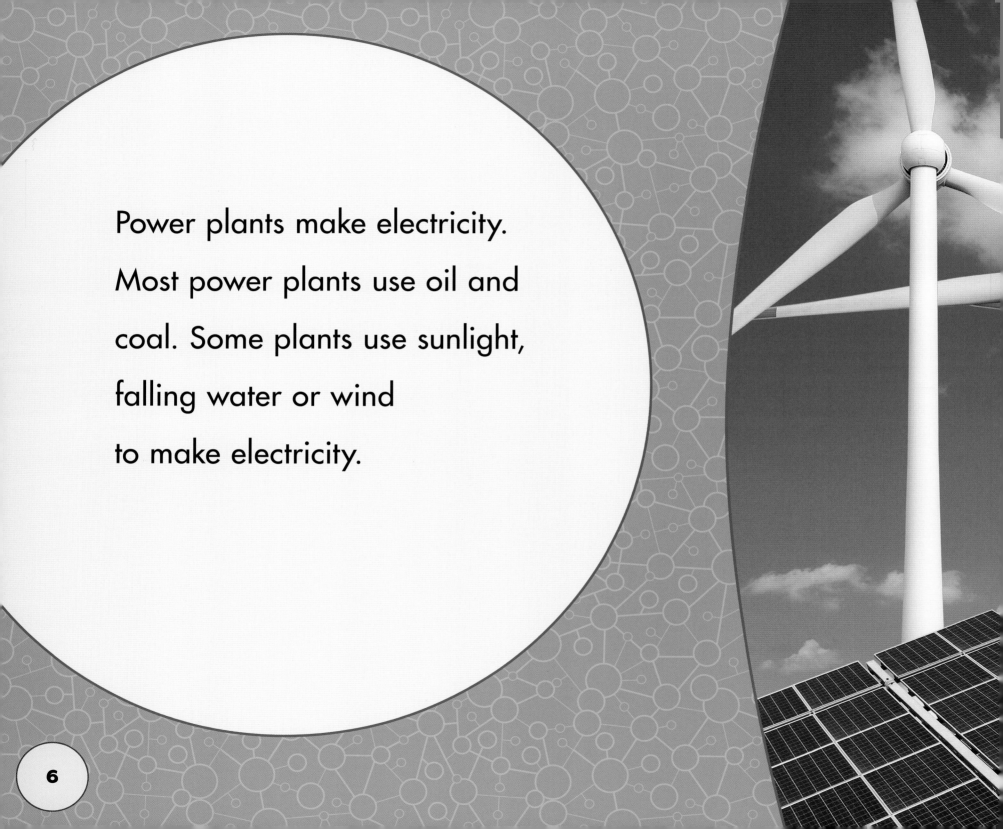

Power plants make electricity. Most power plants use oil and coal. Some plants use sunlight, falling water or wind to make electricity.

How electricity works

Most electricity flows through wires made of metal. Metal can conduct electricity. The wires help electricity get from one place to another.

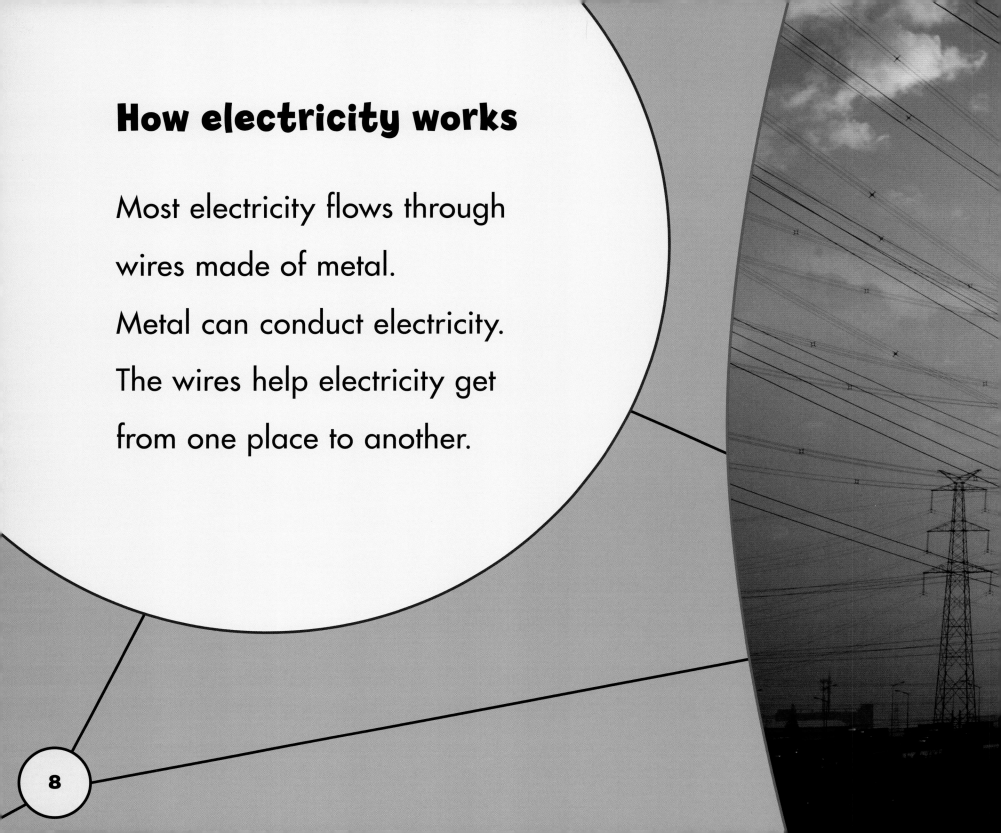

Flipping a switch turns on a light. The switch connects wires in a circuit. Electricity flows in circuits from power plants to wires inside buildings.

Simple electric circuit

BATTERY +

Plastic and rubber are good insulators. Electrical wires are covered with plastic. The plastic makes the electricity flow safely along the wires.

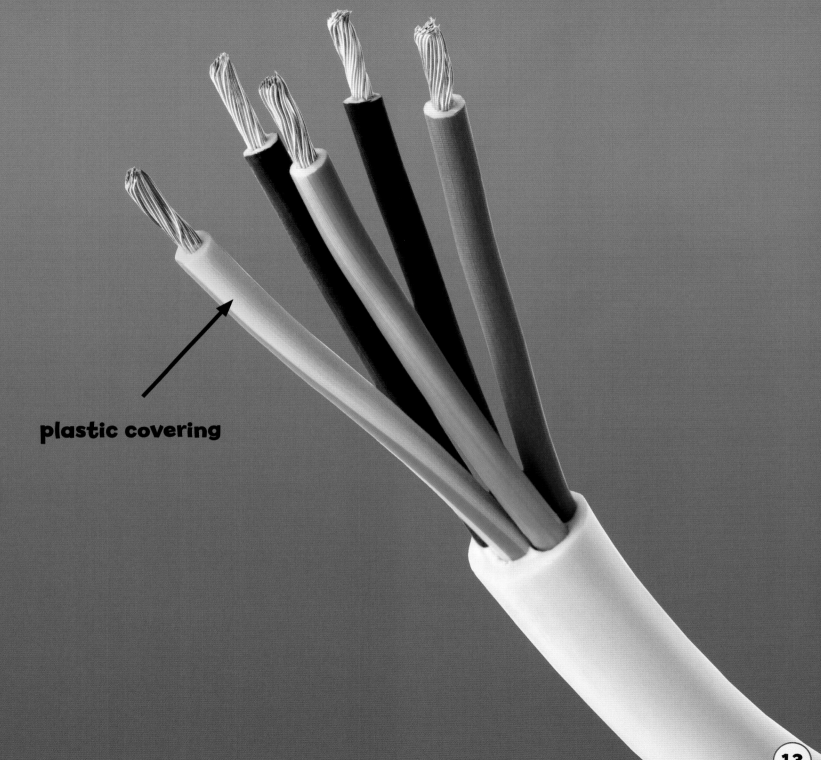

plastic covering

How we use electricity

Electrical energy is used to make light, heat, noise or movement. Many appliances in our homes use electricity. A kettle uses electricity to heat water.

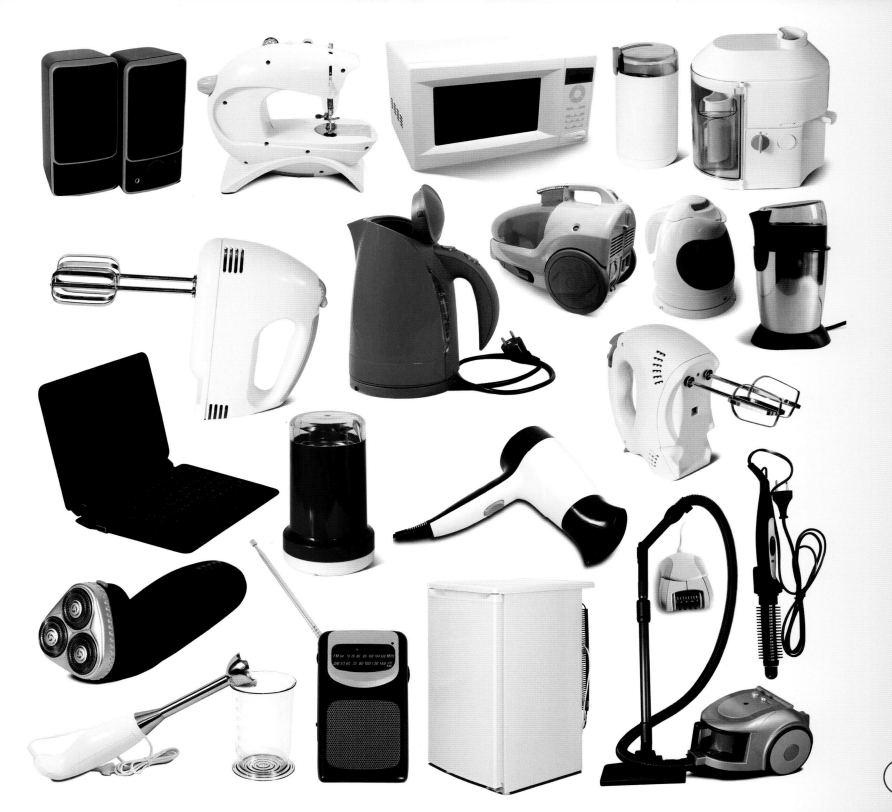

A battery is a store of electricity. Batteries make only a small amount of electricity. They power things very safely.

Static electricity

Rub a balloon on your hair. Your hair moves towards the balloon! Electrons move from your hair to the balloon. They build up and make static electricity.

Activity

If you rub a plastic comb with a woollen cloth, you can cause someone's hair to move. You don't even have to touch the comb to the hair. What other things might move as a result of static electricity? Do the following experiment to find out.

What you need

- plastic comb
- piece of woollen cloth
- inflated balloon
- mixture of salt and pepper
- different kinds of paper such as construction, writing, tissue and wrapping paper
- cotton ball
- aluminum foil
- tooth pick
- small piece of rubber
- mobile phone camera or crayons and paper

What you do

1. Rub the plastic comb with the woollen cloth five times.

2. Bring the comb near to each material. Sort the materials into piles according to whether they move as a result of static electricity.

3. Take or draw a picture to show which items are in each pile.

What do you think?

Make a claim.

A claim is something you believe to be true.

What kind of material is easiest to move with static electricity?

Use the results of your experiment to support your claims.

Glossary

appliance piece of equipment that has a specific purpose

circuit path for electricity to flow through

conductor material that lets heat, electricity or sound travel easily through it; metal is a good conductor of electricity

electron one of the tiny particles that make up all things; protons and neutrons also make up all things

fossil fuel natural fuel formed from the remains of plants and animals; coal, oil, and natural gas are fossil fuels

insulator material that keeps electricity inside wires or paths

static electricity build-up of an electrical charge on the surface of an object

Find out more
Books

Electricity (Moving Up with Science), Peter Riley (Franklin Watts, 2016)

Electricity (Science in Action: How Things Work), Anna Claybourne (QED Publishing, 2016)

How Electricity gets from Power Plants to Homes (Here to There) Megan Cooley Peterson (Capstone Press, 2016)

Websites

resources.woodlands-junior.kent.sch.uk/revision/science/electricity.htm

This site has lots of information, games and activities about electricity.

www.bbc.co.uk/education/clips/zcnhfg8

This video clip shows how electricity travels around Britain.

www.switchedonkids.org.uk/

This site explains how to use electricity safely, with games and quizzes.

Comprehension questions

1. Why are electrical wires usually covered with plastic?

2. Name some appliances you use every day that are powered by batteries.

3. How does electricity get from one place to another?

Index